Clouds of dust billowed on one side of the river. In the dust, dark shapes moved. A Triceratops (try-SEHR-uh-tops) was standing with the rest of his herd by the river's edge.

Triceratops was as long and as tall as a fire truck.
He looked like a giant rhinoceros with his enormous
head and fearsome horns. Triceratops's horns were
so impressive the dinosaur has earned the
nickname Three-Horn.

The dinosaur moved slowly on four thick legs.
As he walked, he held his tail above
the ground. This helped the bulky
creature keep his balance.

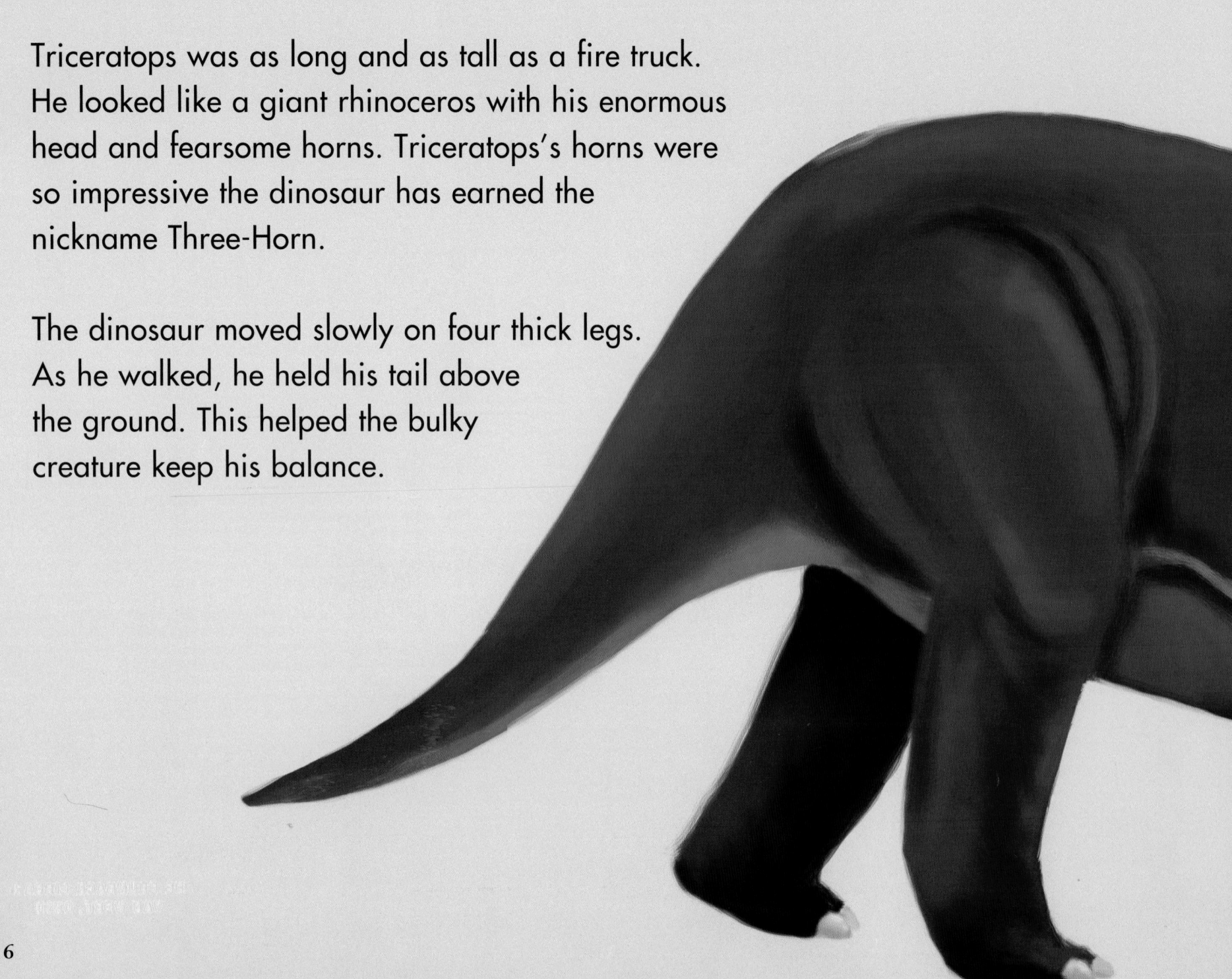

Triceratops was a plant-eater. The creature's sharp teeth and powerful jaws helped grind up tough plants and stems.

Triceratops had sharp teeth near the back of his mouth. The teeth slid past each other like the blades of a scissors. Triceratops had some of the biggest teeth of any plant-eating dinosaur.

Triceratops roamed in large groups for food and safety. That morning, the herd had devoured several acres of ferns in just a few hours. Now all the green plants on their side of the river were gone. But the dinosaurs were still hungry.

With their sturdy feet standing in the river mud, three Triceratops spied more food beyond the water. A forest of cycads swayed in the breeze.

Just as the dinosaurs began to wade across the river, a roar echoed over the plain behind them. A pair of hungry Tyrannosaurus rexes (tuh-RAN-uh-SAWR-us REKS-ez) was following the herd. The dangerous meat-eaters stomped closer and closer. The ground shook with each step.

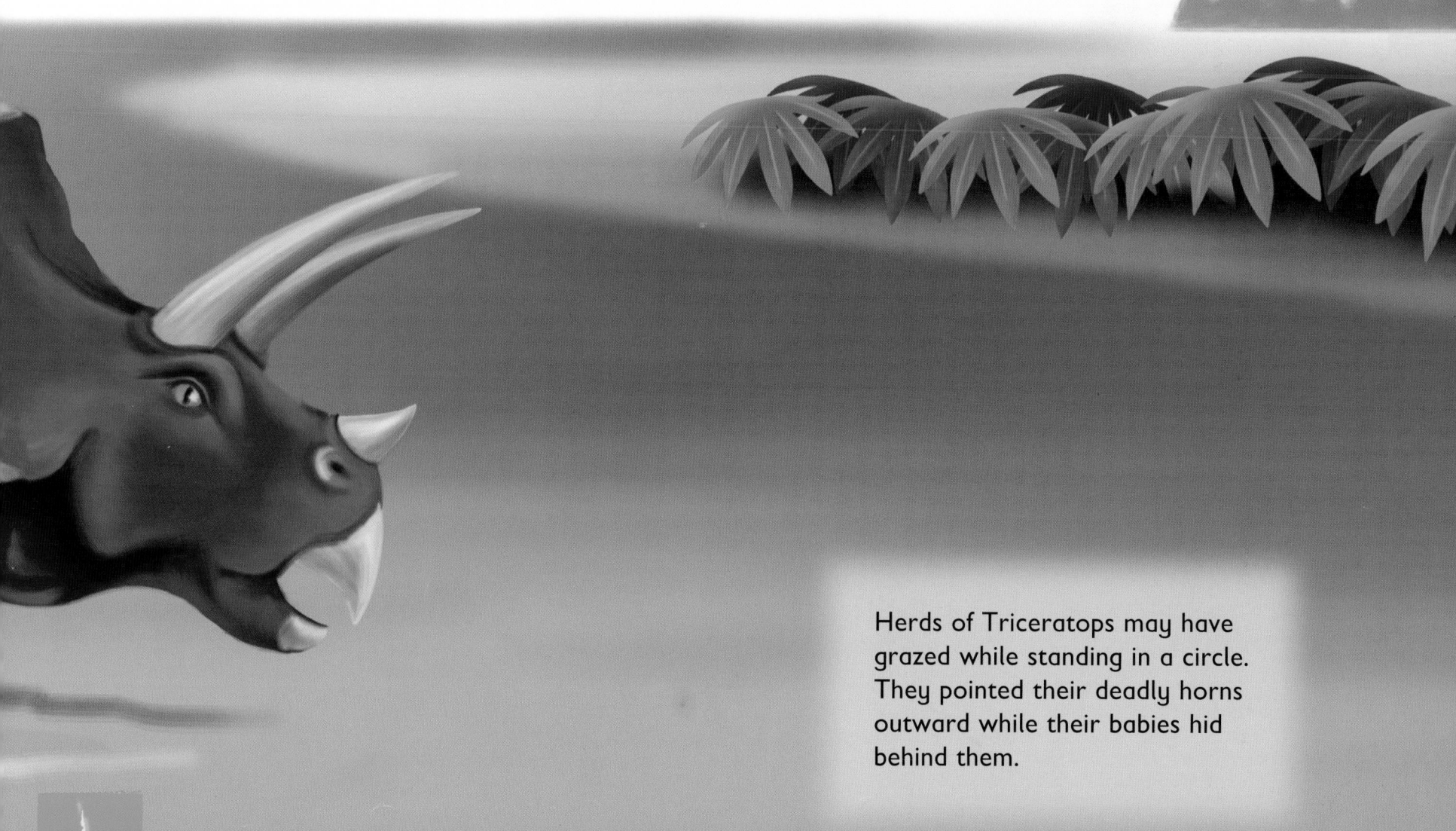

Herds of Triceratops may have grazed while standing in a circle. They pointed their deadly horns outward while their babies hid behind them.

One Tyrannosaurus rex lowered her head and rammed into the side of a young Triceratops. The small plant-eater was stunned.

A row of older Triceratops turned to face their enemy. Their horns, lined up side by side, made a wall of sharp bone. This helped protect the herd.

Triceratops was armed with three heavy horns. Two eyebrow horns grew up to 3 feet (1 meter) long. A third spike, short and thick, poked up just above the creature's snout.

Triceratops had one of the largest heads of any animal that ever walked the earth. It took up one-third of the animal's body.

Two of the biggest Triceratops attacked the tall Tyrannosaurus rex. They lowered their heads and charged like bulls. Their sharp upper horns poked and punched through the predator's tough skin. Their massive heads drove the horns in deep.

An adult Triceratops's head weighed up to 400 pounds (181 kilograms) and was up to 7 feet (2 meters) long.

The other Tyrannosaurus rex joined the battle. He snapped his awesome jaws at a Triceratops's neck. Instead of tasting soft flesh, the predator's teeth clamped down on a ridge of bone.

Triceratops's bony collar also helped balance the back end of the creature's head against his heavy snout and horns. The collar let Triceratops lift his head and move it easily from side to side when feeding or fighting.

The thick, bony collar around the back of the Triceratops's head had protected the plant-eater's neck. This collar was a solid sheet of bone.

The rest of the Triceratops began to panic when they saw the fight. Dozens of the dinosaurs charged into the river. Sprays of water splashed up from stampeding feet. Smaller Triceratops lifted their snouts above the flowing stream.

Triceratops was built like a rhinoceros. Rhinos are the largest land animals that can gallop. Some scientists think that slow-moving Triceratops could gallop at 30 miles (48 kilometers) per hour in a short burst of speed.

19

In the purplish dusk, evening stars sparkled in the sky. The Triceratops herd grazed on the far side of the wide, shallow river. Their turtle-like beaks chomped and chewed the tender cycad leaves.

On the other side of the river, the Tyrannosaurus rex lay lifeless on the ground. Her ferocious companion turned away from the river in search of easier prey.

Triceratops: Where ...

In the United States, Triceratops fossils have been found in Montana, North Dakota, South Dakota, Wyoming, and Colorado. In Canada, they have been found in Alberta and Saskatchewan. Triceratops is the state dinosaur of South Dakota and Wyoming.

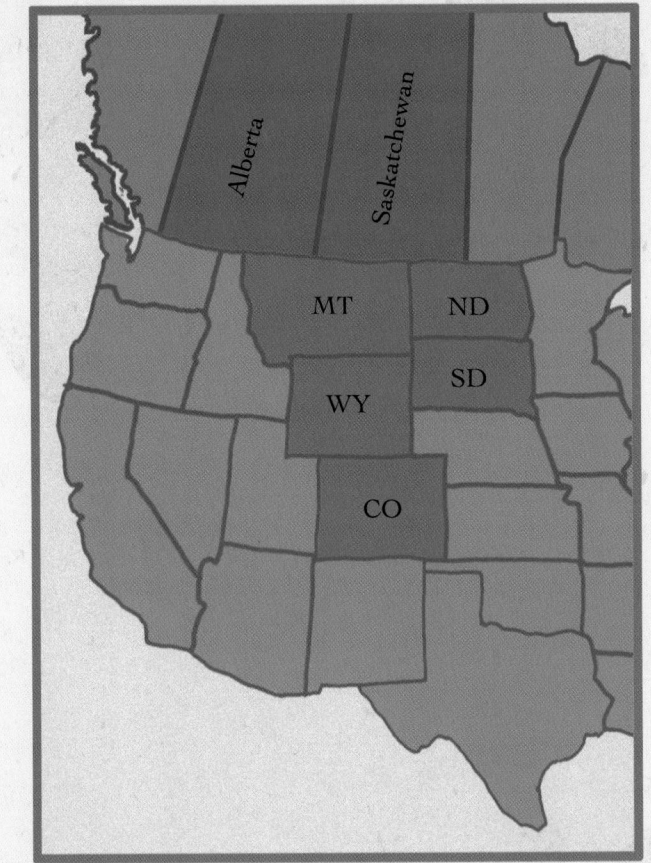

... and When

The "Age of Dinosaurs" began 248 million years ago (mya). If we imagine the time from the beginning of the dinosaur age to the present as one day, dinosaurs lived almost 18 hours—and humans appeared just 10 minutes ago!

Triassic—Dinosaurs first appear. Early mammals appear.
Jurassic—First birds appear.
Cretaceous—Flowering plants appear. By the end of this era, all dinosaurs disappear.

—When Triceratops lived

—First humans appear

22

Digging Deeper

Extra Teeth

The sharp, scissor-like teeth of Triceratops sometimes wore out or broke off. When this happened, new teeth replaced the old ones. Triceratops teeth grew in stacks of three. That gave every tooth at least two replacements.

Tyrannosaurus Treat

Tyrannosaurus rex was the major predator at the time Triceratops lived. Scientists in Saskatchewan, Canada, have discovered fossils of Tyrannosaurus rex droppings. The droppings contain pieces of bone from a Triceratops collar.

Giant Cow

Triceratops sometimes is called the Cow of the Cretaceous, because it grazed in vast herds and ate low-lying green plants, as modern-day cattle do. A single Triceratops weighed as much as 14 modern-day cows, about 14,000 pounds (6,350 kilograms).

Bone Beds

Triceratops is a type of dinosaur called a Ceratopsian (sehr-uh-TOPS-ee-un), or "horned-face" dinosaur. Scientists have found huge collections of Ceratopsian fossils in western Canada and the United States. These groups of fossils are known as bone beds. Giant bone beds of the same kinds of fossils mean the creatures were probably herd animals that lived and died together.

Last Dinosaur

Triceratops was probably the last dinosaur to roam the planet. It lived during the final years of the Age of Dinosaurs.

Words to Know

cycad—a plant shaped like a tall pineapple, with a feathery crown of palm-like leaves
dinosaur—a land reptile that lived in prehistoric times. All dinosaurs died out millions of years ago.
fern—a leafy, flowerless plant
fossil—the remains of a plant or animal that lived between thousands and millions of years ago
predator—an animal that hunts and eats other animals for food
stampede—a sudden wild rush of a frightened herd of animals

To Learn More

At the Library

Bergen, Lara Rice. *Triceratops*. Austin, Tex.: Steadwell Books, 2000.

Cohen, Daniel. *Triceratops*. Mankato, Minn.: Bridgestone Books, 2001.

Landau, Elaine. *Triceratops*. New York: Children's Press, 1999.

On the Web

Enchanted Learning: Zoom Dinosaurs

http://www.EnchantedLearning.com/subjects/dinosaurs

For information, games, and jokes about dinosaurs, fossils, and prehistoric life

The Natural History Museum, London: Dino Directory

http://flood.nhm.ac.uk/cgi-bin/dino

For an alphabetical database of information on the Age of Dinosaurs

University of California, Berkeley: Museum of Paleontology

http://www.ucmp.berkeley.edu/museum/k-12.html

Online exhibits, articles, activities, and resources for teachers and students

Fact Hound

Fact Hound offers a safe, fun way to find Web sites related to this book. All of the sites on Fact Hound have been researched by our staff.

http://www.facthound.com

1. Visit the Fact Hound home page.

2. Enter a search word related to this book, or type in this special code: 1404801367.

3. Click on the FETCH IT button.

Your trusty Fact Hound will fetch the best sites for you!